It's In the Bag!

20 Complete Literature Bags and Centers

Karen A. Moran

UpstartBooks™

Published by UpstartBooks
W5527 State Road 106
P.O. Box 800
Fort Atkinson, Wisconsin 53538-0800
1-800-448-4887

© Karen A. Moran, 2006
Cover design: Debra Neu

Contents

Introduction

It's In the Bag! 20 Complete Literature Bags and Centers provides teachers and librarians with comprehensive lesson plans and reproducible games for 20 popular children's books. The games and lesson plans are cost-effective and simple to construct, and the lesson plans are written with concise directions that are easy to understand.

Literature bags make reading fun for children because each lesson includes a game that is directly related to the topic of the selected book. Literature bags are also user-friendly for librarians and teachers because all of the needed materials can be conveniently organized in bags of your choice.

Lesson Plans

The lesson plans include the following components, which are necessary for developing successful lifetime readers:

- phonemic awareness
- alphabetic principle
- fluency
- comprehension
- vocabulary development
- word recognition

Phonemic Awareness

Phonemic awareness is the ability to hear and manipulate the sounds in spoken words and the understanding that spoken words and syllables are made up of sequences of speech sounds. Phonemic awareness is important because it requires students to notice how letters represent sounds and it gives students a way to approach sounding out new words. The reproducible games and activities in this book provide phonemic awareness reinforcement for your students.

Alphabetic Principle

Alphabetic principle is the understanding that words in spoken language are represented in print and that sounds in words relate to the letters that represent them. Alphabetic principle includes letter-sound recognition, which leads to the ability to use letter-sound correspondence in identifying words. Students will practice alphabetic principle in each lesson when they manipulate the letter tiles to form the provided words.

Fluency

Fluency is the ability to translate letters to sounds to words fluently and effortlessly. When students become fluent, their reading becomes automatic and their attention is focused on comprehension rather than on decoding. Each lesson plan provides a fluency builder to increase reading fluency.

Comprehension

Comprehension is the ability to understand the meaning of written words and to be able to make personal connections with the text. Practicing only literal comprehension skills is not sufficient in developing good readers. The comprehension practice provided in this book reinforces critical and analytical thinking skills. The comprehension stimulators require the student to use higher order thinking skills.

Vocabulary Development

Vocabulary is the sum of words used by, understood by, or at the command of a particular person. The lesson plans in this book include a list of words for students to form by manipulating letter tiles. Students who become adept at forming the given words should be encouraged to form additional words of their choice.

Word Recognition

Word recognition is the ability to automatically recognize written words in a text. Each lesson plan has a challenge word, which the student is required to identify and locate in the story. Being able to recognize words in text leads to increased fluency, which consequently improves comprehension skills.

How to Use Literature Bags in Your Library or Classroom

Literature bags can be used in a variety of ways.

- **Learning Centers.** Literature bags can be stored in a special reading corner or area of the classroom. Give students the opportunity to visit the "Literature Bag Center" for

  - guided reading group assignments

  - enrichment activities or assignments

  - remedial instruction

  - free-time reward

  - good behavior reward

  A sample assignment sheet is provided on page 106.

- **Extended Day or Summer Programs.** Increasingly, schools have been providing extended day and/or summer programs for at-risk students. The literature bag activities in this book are structured to reinforce reading skill development.

- **Lending Libraries.** Give students the opportunity to borrow the literature bags so they can take them home to share with a member of their family.

Parents and relatives serve as valuable resources to help reinforce reading skills at home and to promote the importance and enjoyment of reading. Allowing the students to take the bags home also helps keep families informed of the skills that are covered in the classroom.

- **Tutoring Programs.** Volunteers can easily be trained to use literature bags in a tutoring program. They can also assist the teacher by recording observations and student progress. (A progress chart is also provided on page 106.) Parents, library aides, classroom aides, peer-tutors and high school helpers could serve as volunteers.

- **Preschool Programs.** Societal and governmental pressures have been placed on day care and preschool facilities to aggressively prepare children academically for kindergarten. Literature bags can be an instructional component of a preschool program.

- **Incentive Programs.** Challenge students to complete all 20 literature bags. The following are examples of reward incentives:

  - certificates presented at an awards program (see page 107)

  - a book of the student's choice

  - stickers or sticker charts

  - fast-food coupons donated by local restaurants

  - bowling, miniature golf, movie coupons

  - field trip to a local library or bookstore

Tips for Making Literature Bags

- Purchase pre-fabricated bags or use any large plastic bag—preferably with a zip-lock or drawstring at the opening.

- Whenever possible, laminate the game pieces, letter tiles and lesson plans for durability purposes.

- Glue the lesson plans on a 5" x 8" card; front and back.

- Store the letter tiles in a sandwich-sized ziplock bag.

- Keep the literature book, letter tiles, and game pieces in individual, labeled bags. Instruct the students to always check that there are seven letter tiles before they return the literature bag. When a bag is returned, check the materials section of the lesson plan and account for all game pieces before the bag returns to circulation.

- Designate a specific area of the library or classroom to house the literature bags. Organize them according to your needs. For example:

  - alphabetical by author

  - alphabetical by title

  - alphabetical by skill

  - by skill sequence

- Create a borrowing system. See the sample chart on page 105.

- Create a completion checklist, which can be used for an incentive program. A sample can be found on page 106.

How to Use the Lesson Plans

Read the lesson plan first to familiarize yourself with the skill being taught and the directions for the game that reinforces the skill. Make sure all of the materials are in the bag. There should always be seven letter tiles for the Word Challenge activity. Read the book with your student. Point out the title and the author and illustrator names.

Format of the Lesson Plans

- **Title**

- **Author**

- **Summary.** A brief synopsis of the book.

- **Skill.** Reinforces either phonemic awareness or alphabetic principle. (See a description of these skills on page 5.)

- **Materials.** A list of the materials needed to play the skill game. The game pieces included in the materials listing are reproducible. You might want to color the game pieces or reproduce them on colored paper. You can also laminate them for durability.

- **Directions.** The directions are written so that volunteers, parents and tutors will easily understand how to play the games.

- **Answer Key**

- **Comprehension Stimulators.** Three comprehension questions are provided. The majority of the questions require the student to use higher order thinking skills. It is never too soon to start having children think out of the box. Students who are required to use critical and analytical comprehension skills will perform better on standardized tests and will become accomplished and successful readers. The answers to the questions will vary. Take this opportunity to discuss alternative answers and explore varying opinions with the student. Feel free to ask your own questions to stimulate discussion and improve comprehension.

- **Fluency Builder.** Fluency improves when students read and re-read passages. For most of the activities, the adult will be reading and the student will be providing a missing word or echoing the words read in the story. However, if the student is capable of reading more words, encourage him or her to participate as much as possible.

- **Word Challenge.** Each story has seven letter tiles. Spread the letter tiles out, then say the words listed on the lesson plan and have the student help you manipulate the letter tiles to spell the word. Young children will certainly need assistance with this task. However, at this stage of reading development, it is not important for the students to know how to spell and form the word. The focus should be on having the student understand that letters make sounds and they go together to make words. This is also an excellent opportunity for students to practice letter recognition skills and letter sounds, and to help build vocabulary.

- **Challenge Word.** The challenge word uses all seven letters and can be found at least one time in the story. After discovering the challenge word and arranging the letter tiles to form the word, have the student count the number of times that the word can be found in the story. Show the student how to locate the challenge word by starting at the beginning of the story and using your finger to scan the sentences from left to right until the word is found. Continue this process until the end of the story. This activity increases fluency, word recognition and concept of print.

Note: Some of these activities may be difficult for students who are learning to read—adjust the activities and give assistance as needed so these students are not frustrated. When given encouragement and enthusiasm, most students will be able to experience some measure of success at mastering the skills.

List of Books and Reading Skills

Book	Author	Reading Skills
Are You My Mother?	P. D. Eastman	Syllable Segmentation
Blueberries for Sal	Robert McCloskey	Final Sound Isolation
Brown Bear, Brown Bear, What Do You See?	Bill Martin Jr.	Long Vowels
Caps for Sale	Esphyr Slobodkina	Phoneme Segmentation
Chicka Chicka Boom Boom	John Archambault and Bill Martin Jr.	Matching Upper-/Lowercase Letters
Corduroy	Don Freeman	Syllable Deletion
Good Dog, Carl	Alexandra Day	Blending On-set Rime
Goodnight Moon	Margaret Wise Brown	Rhyme Recognition
Guess How Much I Love You	Sam McBratney	Isolation of Medial Phonemes (short vowels)
Harold and the Purple Crayon	Crockett Johnson	Letter Naming Fluency—Uppercase Letters
If You Give a Mouse a Cookie	Laura Joffe Numeroff	Phoneme Blending
Leo the Late Bloomer	Robert Kraus	Sentence Segmentation
The Little Engine that Could	Watty Piper	Letter Recognition/ABC Order—Uppercase Letters
Mouse Paint	Ellen Stoll Walsh	Phoneme Isolation—Initial Sounds
The Napping House	Audrey Wood	Short Vowel Sounds
One Fish, Two Fish, Red Fish, Blue Fish	Dr. Seuss	Rhyme Production
The Rainbow Fish	Marcus Pfister	Phoneme Deletion
The Snowman	Raymond Briggs	Syllable Blending/Compound Words
The Very Hungry Caterpillar	Eric Carle	Letter Recognition/ABC Order—Lowercase Letters
Where the Wild Things Are	Maurice Sendak	Letter Naming Fluency/Lowercase Letters

Are You My Mother?

Lesson Plan

Are You My Mother?
by P. D. Eastman

Summary

Baby bird hatches from his egg while mother bird is out searching for worms. He goes on a desperate search for his mother and mistakenly believes that everything he sees is his mother.

Skill: Syllable Segmentation

The student will identify the number of syllables in spoken words.

Materials

- 3 nests
- 15 eggs

Directions

Choose an egg. Decide how many syllables are in the word that is represented by the picture on the egg. Place the egg in the nest with the corresponding number of dots. Continue picking eggs until the nests are full.

Answer Key

One syllable—dog, car, boat, frog, book

Two syllables—apple, pencil, pumpkin, glasses, turtle

Three syllables—banana, piano, hamburger, elephant, computer

Comprehension Stimulators

1. How would you feel if you were the little bird who fell out of his nest?
2. Why did the little bird think that everything he met was his mother?
3. Why was "Snort" so important in the story?

Fluency Builder

Read the story aloud. Omit one word from each page and have the student provide the missing word. Reread the story and omit two words from each page. Have the student say the missing words. Continue omitting one additional word as time allows.

Word Challenge

Use the letter tiles to form the following words:

hot	rot	shot	those	them
some	home	toe	set	

Challenge Word: mothers

Count the number of times the word "mothers" can be found in the story.

Are You My Mother? Letter Tiles

m	o	t
h	e	r
s		

Blueberries for Sal

Lesson Plan

Blueberries for Sal
by Robert McCloskey

Summary

Little Sal and her mother are picking blueberries on Blueberry Hill. Little Bear and his mother are also hunting for blueberries. Little Sal and Little Bear get so involved searching for blueberries that they don't realize they have become lost until they cannot find their own mothers.

Skill: Final Sound Isolation

The student will isolate and produce the final sound in a spoken word.

Materials

- 20 blueberries
- 2 pails

Directions

Explain that Little Sal ends with an /l/ sound and Little Bear ends with an /r/ sound. Say one of the words listed in the answer key. The student must repeat the word and then say only the final sound in the word. If the word ends with an /l/ sound, the student places a blueberry in Little Sal's pail. If the word ends with an /r/ sound, the student places a blueberry in Little Bear's pail. Continue until all of the blueberries are placed in the correct pails.

Answer Key

Sal's pail—girl, ball, hill, pull, bell, pail, yell, tail, whale, small

Bear's pail—car, floor, chair, star, fur, fair, near, door, hair, deer

Comprehension Stimulators

1. How were Little Bear and Little Sal alike/different?
2. Why did Little Bear and Little Sal follow the wrong mothers?
3. Was there any part of this story that could not have been real?

Fluency Builders

Practice the phrase, "kerplink, kerplank, kerplunk." Every time the student says one of these words, he or she should drop an object in an aluminum can or pot. (Possible objects could be grapes, peanuts, crayons, etc. Use an object that will make a sound similar to the sound a blueberry would make as it drops into a metal pail.) Reread the story aloud and have the student say, "kerplink, kerplank, kerplunk," and drop the objects into a can/pot.

Word Challenge

Use the letter tiles to form the following words:

led	shed	hut	shut	us
dust	use	let	set	

Challenge Word: hustled

Count the number of times "hustled" can be found in the story.

Blueberries for Sal Reproducibles

Blueberries for Sal Letter Tiles

h	u	s
t	l	e
d		

Brown Bear, Brown Bear, What Do You See?

Lesson Plan

Brown Bear, Brown Bear, What Do You See?
by Bill Martin Jr.

Summary

This colorful rhyming book begins with Brown Bear seeing a red bird. Each animal continues the story by seeing another character until all of the animals are repeated at the conclusion of the book.

Skill: Long Vowels

The student will identify and produce the long vowel sound in a word.

Materials

- glasses (make 5 copies)
- 10 picture circles (lenses)

Directions

Use the following dialogue throughout the game:

You: "_____, _____, *(Say the student's first name twice.)* What do you see?"

The student must then find two pictures that have the same long vowel sound and place each one on the lenses of one of the glasses. Then the student answers with:

Student: "I see a _____ and a _____ looking at me."

Continue until all of the lenses have been placed in the glasses. (You might need to repeat the names of the pictures often to make it easier for the student to discriminate the sounds.)

Answer Key

/e/	bee sheep	/a/	cake tail
/i/	fire kite	/o/	nose bone
/u/	mule cube		

Comprehension Stimulators

1. Which animals in the story would probably not get along with each other?

2. Where do you think the children were when they saw all of these animals?

3. What could the teacher be thinking at the end of this story?

Fluency Builder

Read the book aloud several times. Then cover the pictures with an index card or paper as you reread the book. Have the student see if he or she can remember the sequence of animals in the story as you read it one more time but omit the animal's name. If he or she forgets an animal, give the student a quick peek at the book.

Word Challenge

Use the letter tiles to form the following words:

at	ate	hate	eat	cheat
cat	rat	hat	reach	

Challenge Word: teacher

Count the number of times "teacher" can be found in the story.

Brown Bear, Brown Bear, What Do You See? Reproducibles

Brown Bear, Brown Bear, What Do You See? **It's In the Bag!**

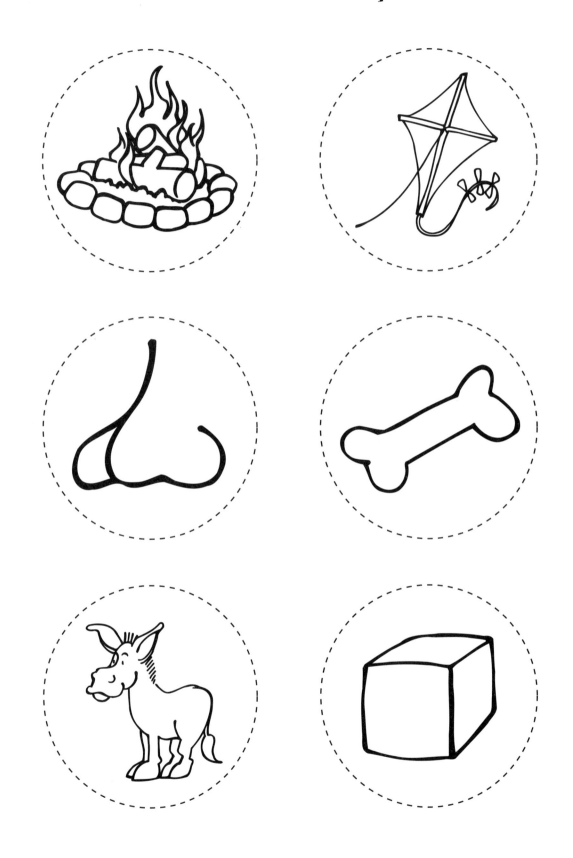

Brown Bear, Brown Bear, What Do You See? Letter Tiles

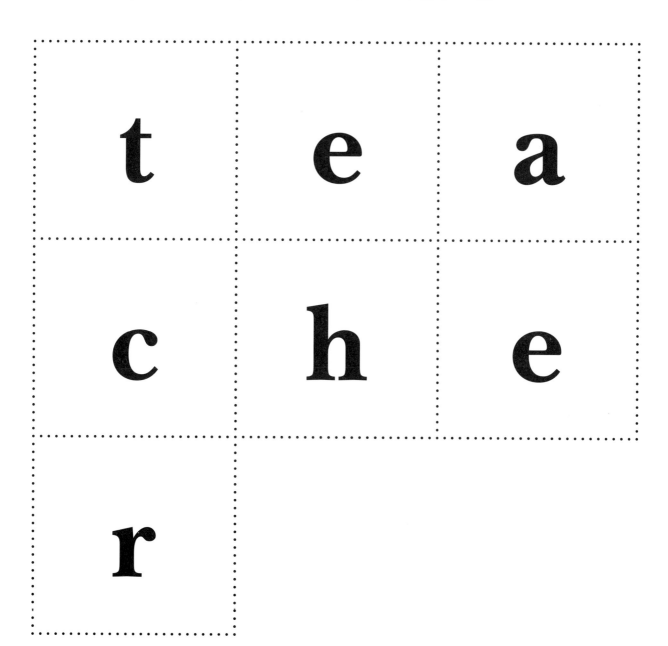

Caps for Sale

Lesson Plan

Caps for Sale
by Esphyr Slobodkina

Summary

A peddler selling caps falls asleep under a tree. When he wakes up, he discovers that monkeys have stolen his caps and won't give them back.

Skill: Phoneme Segmentation

The student will segment individual sounds in given words.

Materials

- 4 monkeys wearing hats
- 1 peddler

Directions

Say each word listed in the answer key. Have the student listen to the word and tell how many phonemes are in the word. Place the peddler on the monkey with the corresponding number of caps. Continue playing the game by determining the number of phonemes in the next word and moving the peddler to the correct monkey.

Answer Key

cap 3	sale 3	back 3	he 2
head 3	I 1	no 2	rest 4
so 2	a 1	brown 4	sleep 4
red 3	time 3	feed 3	

Comprehension Stimulators

1. How did the peddler finally get his caps returned?

2. Why don't we see peddlers selling caps today?

3. How else could the peddler have solved his problem?

Fluency Builder

Read the book aloud. When it is the monkeys' turn to speak, have the student say "Tsz, tsz, tsz." Encourage the student to perform the part by including hand gestures and other movements. Try rereading the book and having the student play the part of the peddler.

Word Challenge

Use the letter tiles to form the following words:

nose	key	men	no	smoke
my	sky	some	money

Challenge Word: monkeys

Count the number of times "monkeys" can be found in the story.

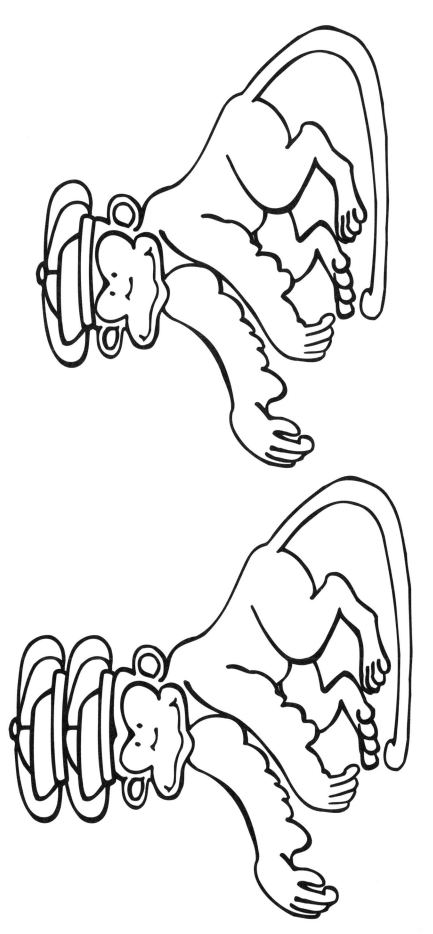

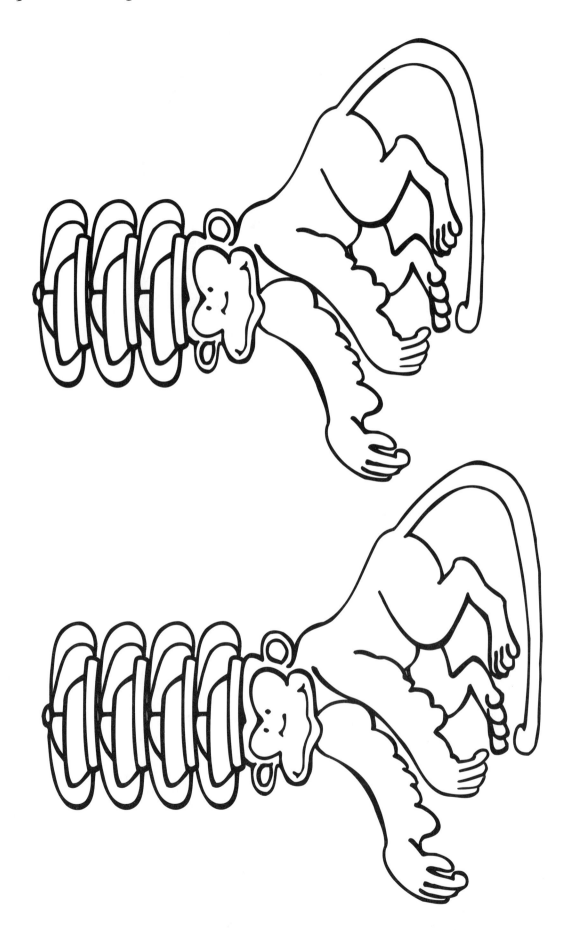

It's In the Bag! Caps for Sale

m	o	n
k	e	y
s		

Chicka Chicka Boom Boom

Lesson Plan

Chicka Chicka Boom Boom
by John Archambault and Bill Martin Jr.

Summary

The letters of the alphabet rush to the top of a coconut tree. But they all come tumbling down … Chicka Chicka Boom Boom!

Skill: Matching Upper-/Lowercase Letters

The student will identify and match uppercase letters with lowercase letters.

Materials

* 4 coconut trees
* 26 coconuts

Directions

Help the coconut letters climb the trees. Choose a coconut. Name the letter and place it on top of the corresponding uppercase letter on the correct coconut tree.

Answer Key

Aa, Bb, Cc, Dd, etc.

Comprehension Stimulators

1. What does "Chicka Chicka Boom Boom" mean?

2. Why did all of the letters follow "a" up the tree?

3. Why did all of the letters fall out of the tree?

Fluency Builder

Line up plastic letters in alphabetical order. Every time you read a letter in the book, point to the corresponding letter and have the student repeat the name of the letter.

Word Challenge

Use the letter tiles to form the following words:

| no | on | to | nut | cut |
| out | cot | not | count | |

Challenge Word: coconut

Count the number of times "coconut" can be found in the story.

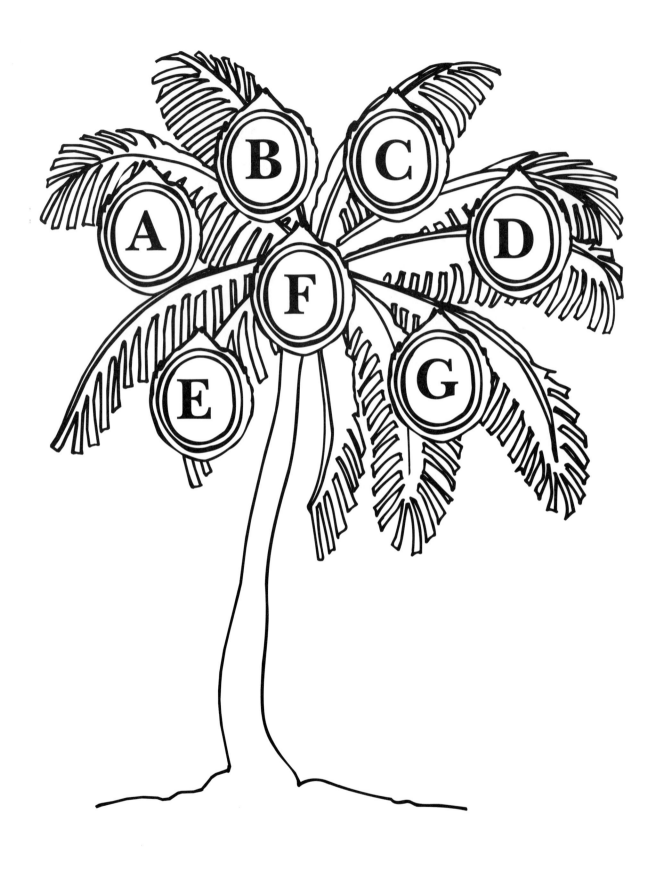

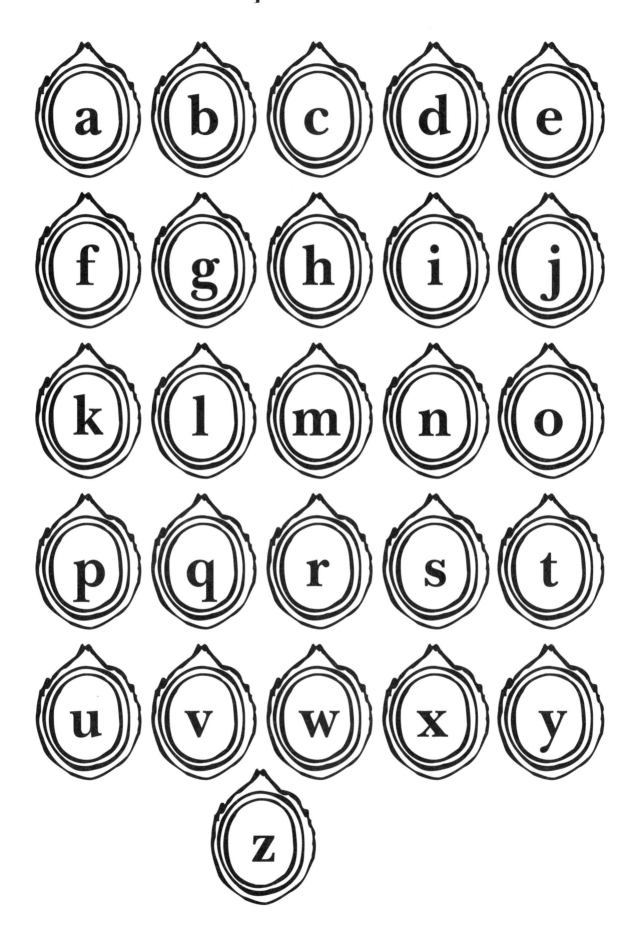

Chicka Chicka Boom Boom Letter Tiles

c	o	c
o	n	u
t		

Corduroy

Lesson Plan

Corduroy
by Don Freeman

Summary

No one wants to buy Corduroy because he has a button missing on his overalls. So the little stuffed bear wanders through the department store searching for the missing button. At last, a little girl comes to Corduroy's rescue and takes him home to be her friend.

Skill: Syllable Deletion

The student will delete the first or second syllable in a two-syllable word.

Materials:

- shopping cart
- 10 toys

Directions

Have the student choose a toy. Continue with the following dialogue:

You: "Panda. *(Name the toy.)* Say 'panda.'"

Student: "Panda."

You: "Say it again but don't say 'pan.'" *(Omit the initial syllable.)*

Student: "Da."

Begin by deleting the initial syllable for each toy. If the student is correct, he or she may place the toy in the shopping cart until all the toys have been purchased. If the student masters deleting the initial syllable, repeat play, deleting the final syllable for each toy.

Answer Key

puzzle	rabbit	yo-yo
football	fire truck	rattle
wagon	airplane	marbles
puppet		

Comprehension Stimulators

1. Why was Corduroy so unhappy in the beginning of the story?

2. Why did the little girl want to buy Corduroy?

3. If you were a toy in the department store, how could you convince someone to buy you?

Fluency Builder

Tape the story of Corduroy on audiocassette. Have the student listen to the story several times. Have the student decide when it is time to turn the pages of the book while he or she is listening to the story on tape.

Word Challenge

Use the letter tiles to form the following words:

but	nut	on	not	tub
sub	sun	bus	bun	

Challenge Word: buttons

Count the number of times "buttons" can be found in the story.

Corduroy Reproducibles

Corduroy Letter Tiles

b	u	t
t	o	n
s		

Good Dog, Carl

Lesson Plan

Good Dog, Carl
by Alexandra Day

Summary

Mother goes shopping and leaves Carl, the trusted family dog, to babysit. While she is gone, Carl entertains the baby and keeps him safe.

Skill: Blending On-set Rime

The student will blend the beginning phoneme and the ending rime to form a word.

Materials

- picture card
- 12 smiley face tokens

Directions

Use the following dialogue throughout the game.

You: "What is this word—/t/ *(pause ½ second)* /op/?"

Student: "Top."

If the student replies correctly, he or she may place a smiley face token on the corresponding picture. Continue until the picture card is covered with tokens. Use the words provided in the answer key.

Answer Key

/b/ /aby/	/d/ /og/	/b/ /ear/
/r/ /ug/	/b/ /ed/	/m/ /om/
/b/ /utter/	/c/ /ookie/	/h/ /at/
/m/ /ilk/	/t/ /ank/	/t/ /ub/

Comprehension Stimulators

1. Do you think the mother should have left the baby alone with Carl? Why or why not?

2. What else could have happened while the mother was gone?

3. What makes Carl a "good dog"?

Fluency Builders

Have the student "read" the book by telling you in his or her own words what he or she thinks is happening on each page.

Word Challenge

Use the letter tiles to form the following words:

lot	lots	rot	hot	shot
shy	try	toy	short	

Challenge Word: shortly

Count the number of times the word "shortly" can be found in the story.

Good Dog, Carl Reproducibles

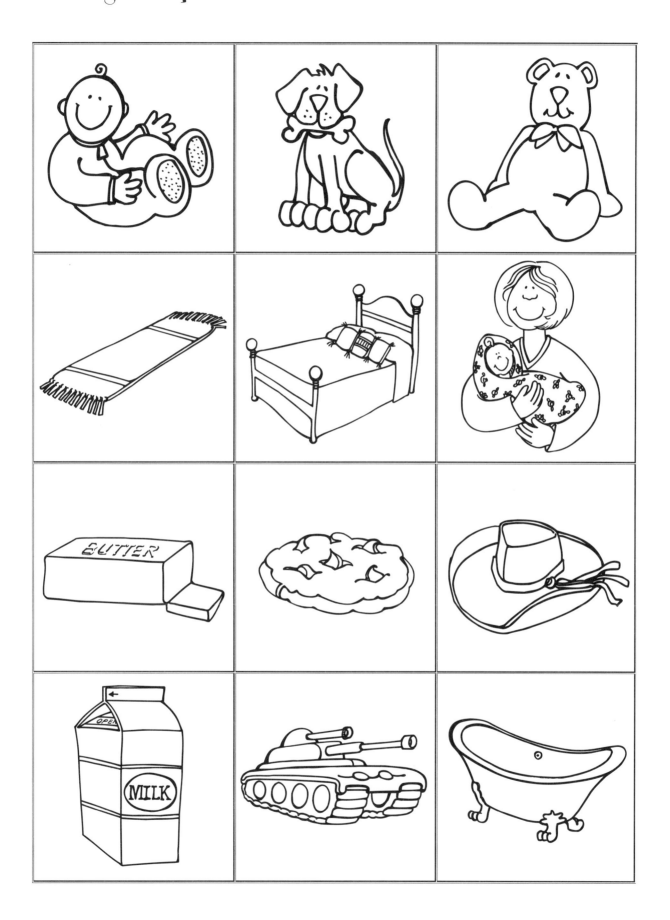

s	h	o
r	t	l
y		

Goodnight Moon

Lesson Plan

Goodnight Moon
by Margaret Wise Brown

Summary

A little bunny prepares for bedtime. As he is lying in his bed, he says goodnight to everything around him.

Skill: Rhyme Recognition

The student will identify pairs of rhyming words.

Materials

- a path of rhyming word pictures leading to a bed
- a bunny
- 10 rhyming word pictures

Directions

Help the bunny get to bed by moving him one "hop" closer each time you find a picture card that rhymes with the next picture along the path.

Answer Key

moon, balloon	bear, chair
kitten, mitten	bat, hat
clock, sock	house, mouse
star, car	rug, bug
phone, bone	yarn, barn

Comprehension Stimulators

1. Why does bunny want to say goodnight to everything?
2. Who do you think the old lady is?
3. Name something else bunny could do to get ready for bed.

Fluency Builder

After the story has been read several times, turn the lights out and use a flashlight to read the bedtime story. Every time you read the words "goodnight _____" flash the light on the object in the book and have the student complete the phrase.

Word Challenge

Use the letter tiles to form the following words:

it	kite	net	tent	sit
kit	ten	sent	tin	

Challenge Word: kittens

Count the number of times "kittens" can be found in the story.

Goodnight Moon Reproducibles

Goodnight Moon Reproducibles

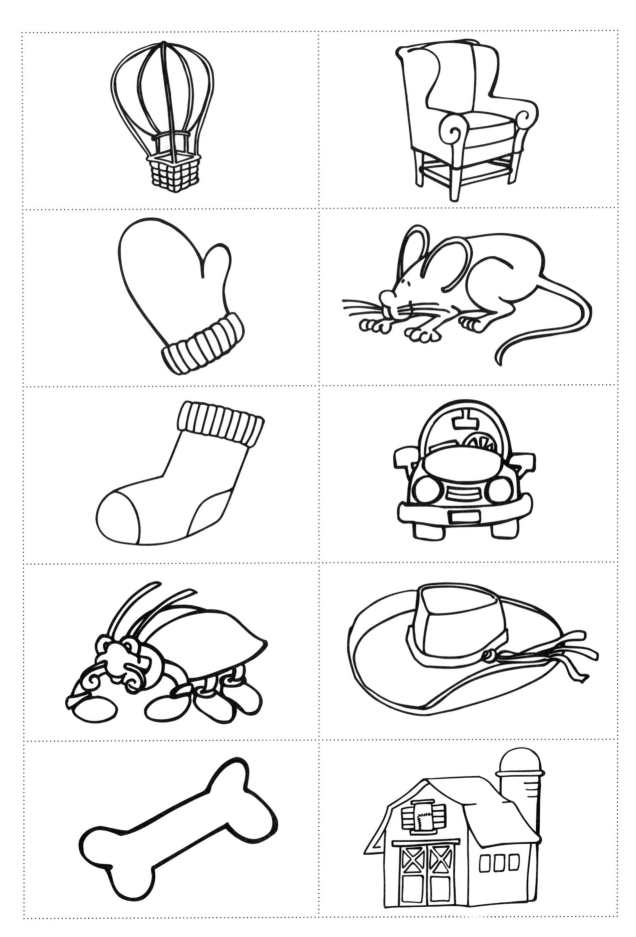

Goodnight Moon Letter Tiles

k	i	t
t	e	n
s		

Guess How Much I Love You

Lesson Plan

Guess How Much I Love You
by Sam McBratney

Summary

Little Nutbrown Hare searches for the perfect way to tell Big Nutbrown Hare how much he loves him.

Skill: Isolation of Medial Phonemes (short vowels)

The student will isolate and say the medial phoneme (sound) in a spoken word.

Materials

- Little Nutbrown Hare
- 10 picture cards

Directions

See how far apart Little Nutbrown Hare's paws will stretch to show how much he loves Big Nutbrown Hare. Choose a card. Say the name of the picture. If the student can isolate the medial sound, have him or her place the card between the hare's paws. As he or she continues to answer correctly, have the student place the card between the paws to show how much his or her love is growing. Use the following dialogue:

You: "Say 'bag.'"

Student: "Bag."

You: "Tell me the sound you hear in the middle of the word."

Student: "/A/." *(Short "a" sound.)*

(The student must produce the sound, not the name of the letter.)

Answer Key

pig /i/   box /o/
cup /u/   rat /a/
jet /e/ (the short e sound, not the letter)
jug /u/
bed /e/   map /a/
fox /o/   fish /i/

Comprehension Stimulators

1. Talk about the ways you show people that you love them.

2. Tell about another way Little Nutbrown Hare could have shown that he loved Big Nutbrown Hare.

3. If the hares were turtles, how could they have shown that they loved each other?

Fluency Builder

Read the story aloud and have the student "read" Big Nutbrown Hare's part in the story by echoing the words Little Nutbrown Hare says when he declares his love.

Word Challenge

Use the letter tiles to form the following words:

he	she	her	hers	set
rest	test	chest	the	

Challenge Word: stretch

Count the number of times "stretch" can be found in the story.

sample

Guess How Much I Love You Reproducibles

Guess How Much I Love You Letter Tiles

s	t	r
e	t	c
h		

Harold and the Purple Crayon

Lesson Plan

Harold and the Purple Crayon
by Crockett Johnson

Summary

Harold goes for a walk and creates his own adventures with a purple crayon.

Skill: Letter Naming Fluency–Uppercase Letters

The student will practice becoming fluent in naming the uppercase letters of the alphabet.

Materials

- a clock or watch
- Harold
- the purple crayon
- 26 uppercase letter cards

Directions

Place Harold at the base of the crayon. Note the time on a watch or clock. Flash through the letter cards and have the student name the letters. Record the number of minutes/seconds that pass. Move Harold one step up the purple crayon closer to the top. Review the incorrect/unknown letters with the student. Repeat the same procedure. If the student decreased his or her time, Harold may climb up one step closer. Continue until Harold reaches the top of the crayon.

Answer Key

Times will vary.

Comprehension Stimulators

1. Why is the purple crayon important in this story?

2. Name three things you would have drawn if you were Harold.

3. How would the story have been different if Harold's crayon had fallen overboard when he was in the boat?

Fluency Builder

Have the student count the number of times "purple crayon" is mentioned in the story. Every time you read "purple crayon," have the student hold up a purple crayon.

Word Challenge

Use the letter tiles to form the following words:

in	win	wind	so	no
snow	down	now	wow	

Challenge Word: windows

Count the number of times "windows" can be found in the story.

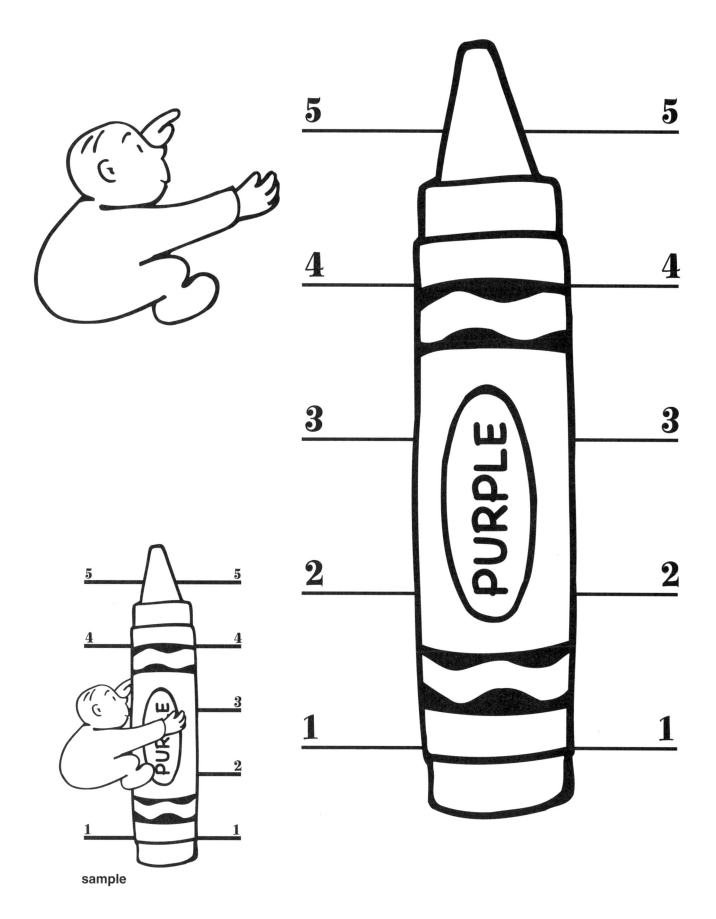

sample

A	B	C	D	E
F	G	H	I	J
K	L	M	N	O
P	Q	R	S	T
U	V	W	X	Y
Z				

Harold and the Purple Crayon Letter Tiles

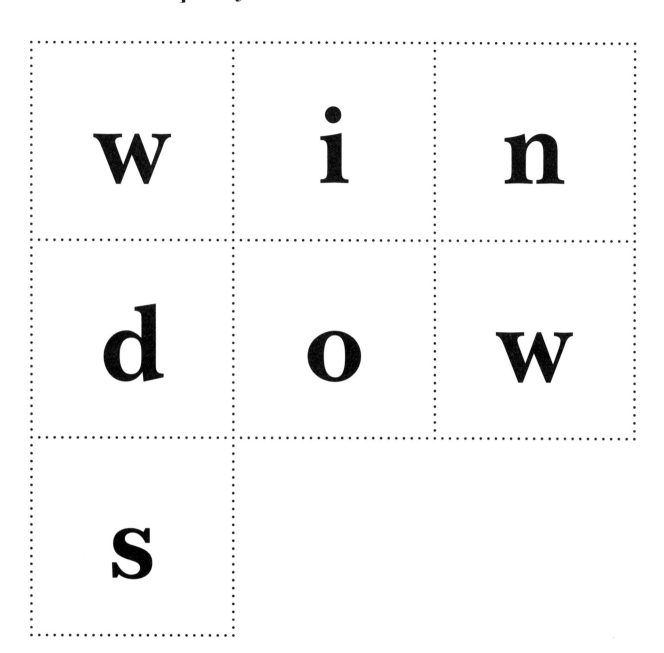

If You Give a Mouse a Cookie

Lesson Plan

If You Give a Mouse a Cookie
by Laura Joffe Numeroff

Summary

One day a little boy is playing outside when he spies a mouse. The boy is generous and offers one of his cookies to the mouse. Trouble begins when the mouse enters the boy's house and is not satisfied with "just" a cookie.

Skill: Phoneme Blending

The student will blend phonemes (sounds) to form a word.

Materials

*   1 cookie jar
*   2 cookies (make 10 copies for a total of 20)
*   1 mouse

Directions

Begin with the first word in the answer key and say the sounds in the word individually. Pause ½ second between each phoneme. If the student can blend the sounds to form the given word, he or she may take a cookie from the jar and give it to the mouse. Continue until the cookie jar is empty.

Answer Key

b-o-x	g-a-me	m-ou-se	b-a-th
n-ai-l	b-i-ke	f-ee-t	h-ou-se
n-a-p	b-e-d	r-ea-d	b-oo-k
f-i-sh	l-igh-t	d-r-aw	p-e-n
k-i-te	c-oa-t	t-e-n	d-ow-n

Comprehension Stimulators

1. How would the story have been different if the mouse were a dog?

2. If you were the boy, would you have been worried when the mouse came in the house? Why or why not?

3. What do you think is going to happen if the boy gives the mouse another cookie?

Fluency Builder

Read the story aloud and choose one word on each page for the student to read. When you reach that word in the story, say "blank." The student must read the missing word to fill in the "blank."

Word Challenge

Use the letter tiles to form the following words:

cup	trip	pie	rice	pet
cute	ripe	tire	tip	

Challenge Word: picture

Count the number of times "picture" can be found in the story.

p	i	c
t	u	r
e		

Leo the Late Bloomer

Lesson Plan

Leo the Late Bloomer
by Robert Kraus

Summary

Leo couldn't seem to do anything right. His mother called him a late bloomer because he couldn't write, read, or draw. Then one day Leo spoke a whole sentence and he "bloomed."

Skill: Sentence Segmentation

The student will identify the number of words in a sentence.

Materials:

- 3 flowerpots
- 10 flowers

Directions

Leo's first sentence was "I made it!" This sentence contains three words. Place one flower in the flowerpot that has three dots. Continue with the sentences in the answer key until each flower is placed in a flowerpot. (It is helpful to have the student clap the number of words in a sentence before saying the number of words.)

Answer Key

He could not read.	4
He never spoke.	3
Leo was sad.	3

He cried.	2
Leo hid.	2
His mom loved him.	4
The snows came.	3
The trees grew leaves.	4
Leo bloomed.	2
He could read.	3

Comprehension Stimulators

1. Why did Leo's dad keep watching him?
2. How do you know that Leo's mother was smart?
3. How does Leo feel at the beginning of the story and at the end of the story?

Fluency Builder

Have the student read the sentences that talk about what Leo could not do. "He couldn't read" … Then have him or her read the sentences at the end about what Leo could do. Count the number of written words in the sentences to reinforce sentence segmentation.

Word Challenge

Use the letter tiles to form the following words:

led   bed   bled   old   bloom
bold   mood   boom   loom

Challenge Word: bloomed

Count the number of times "bloomed" can be found in the story.

Leo the Late Bloomer Letter Tiles

b	l	o
o	m	e
d		

The Little Engine that Could

Lesson Plan

The Little Engine that Could
by Watty Piper

Summary

A train loaded with toys and food for little girls and boys is stuck without an engine to pull it. None of the engines that pass by will stop to help. Then a little blue engine offers to haul the train over the mountain so the boys and girls will not be disappointed.

Skill: Letter Recognition/ABC Order– Uppercase Letters

The student will practice letter recognition by naming the uppercase letters of the alphabet and arranging them in alphabetical order.

Materials

- one engine
- 7 train cars
- 7 letter cards

Directions

Assemble the train by putting the engine and train cars in ABC order. Then put the missing letters in ABC order until the train is complete.

Answer Key

ABC order.

Comprehension Stimulators

1. What else could the toys have done to solve their problem if the little blue engine had not been there to help?

2. What could the children have said or done to show their thanks to the little blue engine?

3. Why did the little blue engine keep trying?

Fluency Builder

Read the story aloud until you come to the dialogue. Read the dialogue with expression and have the student repeat it with you using the same expression. (You may have to group the words into chunks of three to four words to make it easier for the student to remember the words.)

Word Challenge

Use the letter tiles to form the following words:

man	nail	am
is	mail	snail
as	sail	slam

Challenge Word: animals

Count the number of times "animals" can be found in the story.

The Little Engine that Could Letter Tiles

a	n	i
m	a	l
s		

Mouse Paint

Lesson Plan

Mouse Paint
by Ellen Stoll Walsh

Summary

Three white mice have fun climbing into red, yellow, and blue paint jars. As they dance through paint puddles, they discover how new colors can be made.

Skill: Phoneme Isolation—Initial Sounds

The student will discriminate and identify the initial sounds in words.

Materials

- 3 paint jars
- 18 picture cards

Directions

Have the student choose a picture card and name the beginning sound in the word. Place the picture in the jar that has the corresponding beginning sound. Continue identifying the initial sound for each picture and placing it in the correct jar.

Answer Key

Blue jar—balloon, butterfly, bear, barn, boat, bicycle

Yellow jar—yak, yawn, yo-yo, yolk, yard, yarn

Red jar—ring, rake, rocket, rose, raccoon, rabbit

Comprehension Stimulators

1. Why did the mice leave part of the paper white instead of painting it?

2. What else can the mice do with the paints?

3. How would the story have been different if the mice had not taken a bath?

Fluency Builder

Read the story and have the student use a paintbrush to "paint" your words as you read. Explain how the words flow across the page from left to right in a story.

Word Challenge

Use the letter tiles to form the following words:

pan	tin	pen
tan	tap	den
pin	ten	pain

Challenge Word: painted

Count the number of times "painted" can be found in the story.

Color this jar **BLUE**.

Color this jar **YELLOW**.

Color this jar **RED.**

Mouse Paint Reproducibles

Mouse Paint Letter Tiles

p	a	i
n	t	e
d		

The Napping House

Lesson Plan

The Napping House
by Audrey Wood

Summary

Everyone is sleeping in the napping house until a flea bites the mouse and causes such a commotion that everyone in the house wakes up.

Skill: Short Vowel Sounds

The student will say the short vowel sound in a word.

Materials

- 1 house
- 15 picture cards

Directions

Select a picture card. Have the student say the vowel sound heard in the word. Place the picture card on the window that contains a picture with the same vowel sound. Continue choosing picture cards until all of the windows in the house are covered.

Answer Key

apple—pan, bag, can

egg—ten, pen, leg

box—dog, pot, lock

bus—gum, sun, gun

pig—wig, pin, zip

Comprehension Stimulators

1. What else could have woken everyone from his or her sleep?

2. What other title could you give to this story?

3. Would you like to sleep this way in your bed? Why or why not?

Fluency Builder

Build fluency by performing an echo reading—you read a line and have the student echo that line using the same expression. Continue reading each line and having the student echo it.

Word Challenge

Use the letter tiles to form the following words:

or	in	no
ring	on	so
sing	go	song

Challenge Word: snoring

Count the number of times "snoring" can be found in the story.

s	n	o
r	i	n
g		

One Fish, Two Fish, Red Fish, Blue Fish

Lesson Plan

One Fish, Two Fish, Red Fish, Blue Fish
by Dr. Seuss

Summary

Funny animals are displaying strange behaviors in this Dr. Seuss book of rhyming verse.

Skill: Rhyme Production

The student will produce a word that rhymes with a given word. Nonsense words are acceptable.

Materials

- a fish tank
- 10 fish

Directions

Select a fish and say the name of the picture printed on the fish. If the student can produce a rhyming word, place the fish in the fish tank. Continue until all of the fish are in the tank.

Answer Key

Accept any rhyming words, including nonsense words.

Comprehension Stimulators

1. Where do you think "near" and "far" can be found?

2. Which "thing" is your favorite character and why?

3. Create your own "funny thing" and tell how it acts.

Fluency Builder

Read the story again but omit the last word on each page and have the student supply the rhyming word.

Word Challenge

Use the letter tiles to form the following words:

eat	tone	then
heat	note	near
neat	hen	other

Challenge Word: another

Count the number of times "another" can be found in the story.

It's In the Bag! One Fish, Two Fish, Red Fish, Blue Fish

One Fish, Two Fish, Red Fish, Blue Fish Reproducibles

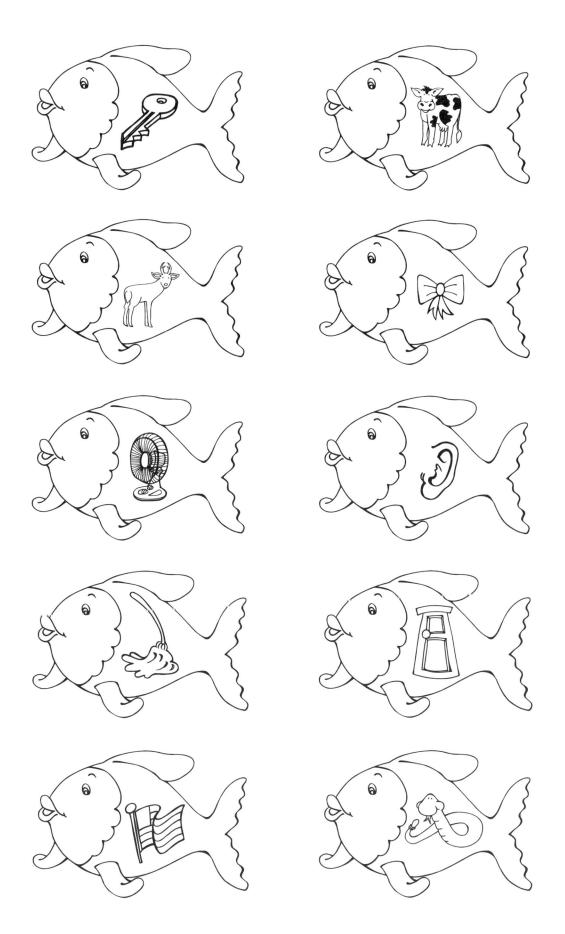

It's In the Bag! One Fish, Two Fish, Red Fish, Blue Fish

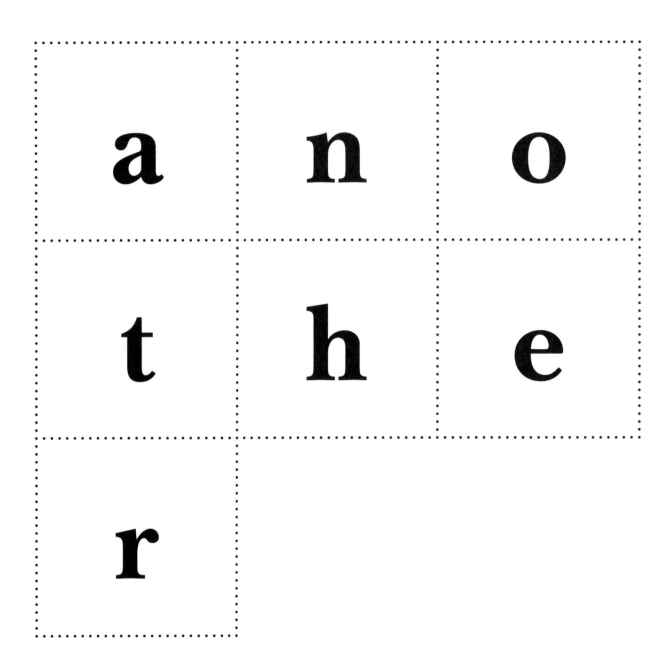

a	n	o
t	h	e
r		

The Rainbow Fish

Lesson Plan

The Rainbow Fish
by Marcus Pfister

Summary

A beautiful fish covered in shimmering scales learns how to make friends by sharing his precious scales with other less fortunate fish.

Skill: Phoneme Deletion

The student will delete the initial/final phoneme in a spoken word.

Materials

- 11 aluminum foil scales (Tip: Cut out the scale. Trace the scale on a piece of foil. Wrap the foil around the paper and tape it together to make it more durable.)

- rainbow fish

- 10 fish

Directions

Place all of the foil scales on the large rainbow fish to begin the game. Scatter the smaller fish around Rainbow Fish. Use the following dialogue for each of the words in the answer key.

You: "Say 'boat.'"

Student: "Boat."

You: "Say it again but don't say /t/." (*Say the sound, not the letter.*)

Student: "Boa."

If the answer is correct, the student may take away one of the Rainbow Fish's scales and give it to another fish. Continue until the Rainbow Fish has only one scale and each of the other fish have one scale.

Answer Key

Say boat—Say it again but don't say /t/.

fish /sh/	friend /d/	swim /m/
boat /b/	scale /l/	fish /f/

(*The last three words are difficult because the student must delete a phoneme from a consonant blend.*)

swim /s/	scale /s/	friend /f/

Comprehension Stimulators

1. What advice did the octopus give to the rainbow fish? Was it good advice? Why or why not?

2. How did Rainbow Fish change throughout the story?

3. What could you do to make friends?

Fluency Builder

Use a piece of aluminum foil as a guide (approximately 6" wide). Place the guide under the first line in the story. As you read aloud, slide the guide down a row under the next line. Explain how this guide helps you keep your place so the story flows when you read it. Continue through the entire book.

Word Challenge

Use the letter tiles to form the following words:

rain	win	air	bow	bar
rob	rain	rib	now	

Challenge Word: rainbow

Count the number of times "rainbow" can be found in the story.

The Rainbow Fish Reproducibles

Cut out the scales and cover them in aluminum foil.

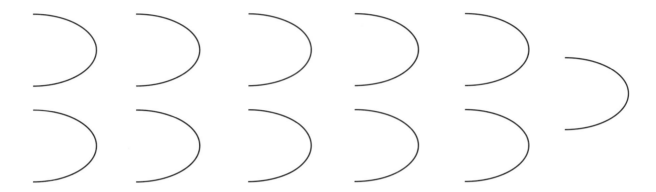

The Rainbow Fish Reproducibles

r	a	i
n	b	o
w		

The Snowman

Lesson Plan

The Snowman
by Raymond Briggs

Summary

One snowy day, James builds a snowman. At night, the snowman comes alive and takes James on a great adventure to a land where the snowman's friends live.

Skill: Syllable Blending/Compound Words

The student will practice blending syllables to form compound words.

Materials

- 1 compound word grid
- 12 picture cards
- 6 compound word picture cards

Glue the pictures to two different colors of construction paper—one for the picture cards and another for the compound word pictures.

Directions

Follow the snowmam example to make new compound words. Spread out the picture cards on a flat surface. Select two picture cards that can be combined to make a compound word. Place the pictures and the compound word picture on the grid.

Answer Key

birdhouse	butterfly
starfish	rainbow
football	cupcake

Comprehension Stimulators

1. What could have happened if James's parents had woken up when the snowman was in the house?

2. What do you think will happen the next time James builds a snowman?

3. What would the snowman tell James if he could talk?

Fluency Builder

Have the student assist you in highlighting every "snow" word in the story. (Highlighting tape is great for this exercise.) Read the story. Every time you find a "snow" word, have the student read the word.

Word Challenge

Use the letter tiles to form the following words:

man	so	now
saw	no	moan
was	snow	swam

Challenge Word: snowman

Count the number of times "snowman" can be found in the story.

The Snowman Reproducibles

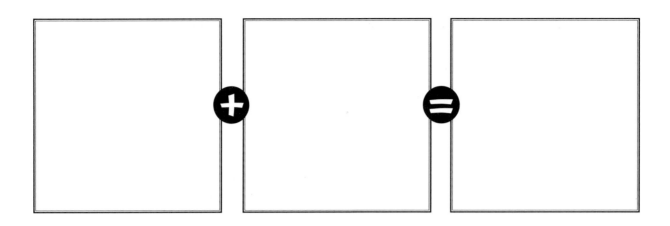

  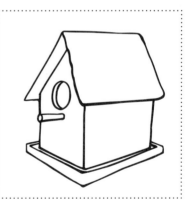

It's In the Bag! The Snowman

The Snowman Reproducibles

s	n	o
w	m	a
n		

⭐ The Very Hungry Caterpillar ⭐

Lesson Plan

The Very Hungry Caterpillar
by Eric Carle

Summary

A hungry caterpillar hatches out of an egg and searches for food. After eating through a variety of foods, he builds a cocoon. Two weeks later, he emerges as a beautiful butterfly.

Skill: Letter Recognition/ABC Order–Lowercase Letters

The student will practice letter recognition by naming the lowercase letters of the alphabet and arranging them in alphabetical order.

Materials

- 10 caterpillar parts

Directions

Make your own hungry caterpillar. Begin with the caterpillar's head. Then arrange the remaining pieces in ABC order until you complete the alphabet and the caterpillar.

Answer Key

ABC order.

Comprehension Stimulators

1. How did the caterpillar change throughout the book?

2. Why did the caterpillar feel better after eating a leaf?

3. Tell a story about "a very hungry butterfly."

Fluency Builder

Have the student identify each letter on the caterpillar, then produce its corresponding sound.

Word Challenge

Use the letter tiles to form the words below. Explain that several of these words will contain a "T" when you form them, which is an incorrect way to use the letter. The capital "T" should only be used at the beginning of a proper noun.

day	dust	yes
say	seat	ate
stay	sad	date

Challenge Word: Tuesday

Count the number of times "Tuesday" can be found in the story.

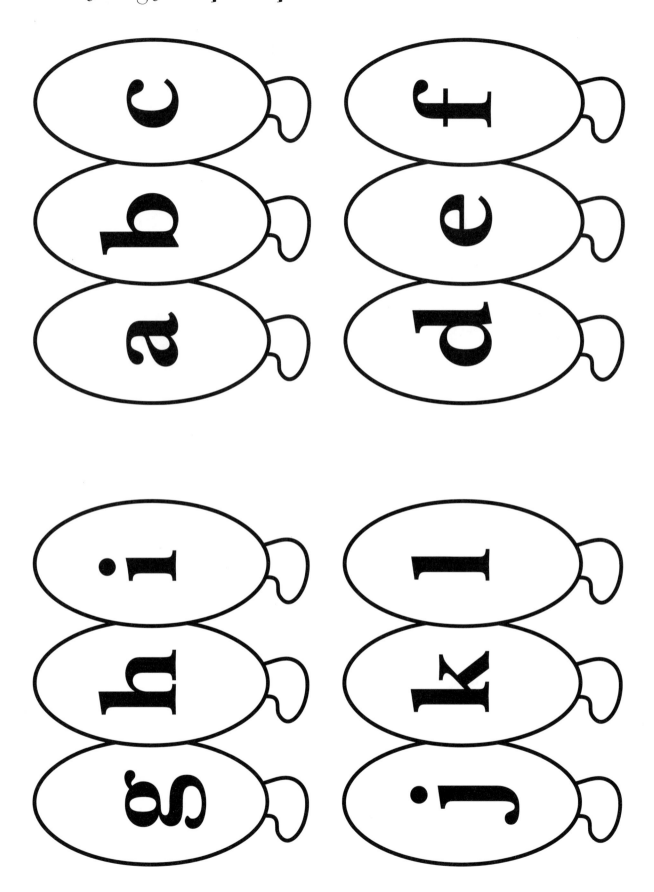

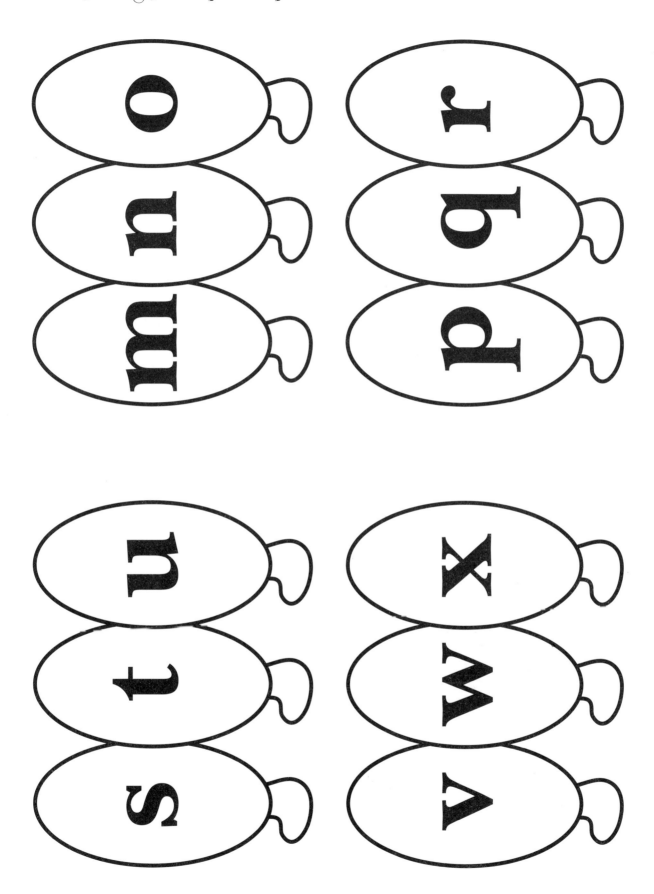

The Very Hungry Caterpillar Letter Tiles

T	u	e
s	d	a
y		

Where the Wild Things Are

Lesson Plan

Where the Wild Things Are
by Maurice Sendak

Summary

Max misbehaves and is sent to his room without supper. He sails far away to the land of the wild things and rules as their king until he becomes lonely and returns home.

Skill: Letter Naming Fluency/Lowercase Letters

The student will practice becoming fluent in naming the lowercase letters of the alphabet.

Materials

- Max in his boat
- forest and wild things strip
- 26 lowercase letter cards

Directions

Make a wave number line like the sample on page 102. Place Max and his boat in the forest. Note the time. Flash through the letter cards and have the student name the letters. Record the number of minutes/seconds that passed. Move Max one spot closer to the wild things. Review the incorrect/unknown letters with the student. Begin timing again as the student names the letters. If the student decreased his or her time, he or she may move one spot closer. Continue until Max reaches his destination.

Answer Key

ABC order.

Comprehension Stimulators

1. What do you think Max's punishment should have been for misbehaving?

2. Why didn't the wild things attack Max?

3. Why was Max's supper still hot when he returned home?

Fluency Builder

Practice repeating the sentence, "The wild things roared their terrible roars and gnashed their terrible teeth and showed their terrible claws." Have the student perform this passage as a wild thing each time it appears in the story.

Word Challenge

Use the letter tiles to form the following words:

gas	sing	star
rain	ring	tag
art	tar	rag

Challenge Word: staring

Count the number of times "staring" can be found in the story.

sample

1   2   3   4   5

a	b	c	d	e
f	g	h	i	j
k	l	m	n	o
p	q	r	s	t
u	v	w	x	y
z				

s	t	a
r	i	n
g		

Classroom Borrowing Chart

Name	Literature Bag	Date Borrowed	Date Returned

Progress Chart

Name:

Name of Completed Literature Bag:

Date Returned:

Comments: *(Please include any observations or comments that would be helpful to the teacher.)*

Signature of Parent or Volunteer:

★ Assignment Sheet ★

After completion, the student should place a check mark in the Student Check box.

Name:

Literature Bag Assigned	Student Check	Teacher Check

Literature Bag Award Certificate

This award is presented to

Name of Student

for successfully completing
all 20 Literature Bags.

Congratulations!

Teacher's Signature and Date